Perfect in His Eyes!

For permission requests, please contact:
Renewed Minds Publishing House
www.theselfcaresanctuary.org

This book is a work of inspiration and encouragement. It is intended to provide general information and biblical guidance and should not replace professional counseling or therapy for individuals in need of support.

Scripture quotations are taken from [Bible Version, e.g., *New International Version (NIV)*], © [2024], used by permission. All rights reserved worldwide.

Printed in the United States of America

ISBN: 979-8-9890139-6-8

Acknowledgements

First and foremost, I give all glory and honor to God, whose unfailing love and guidance made this book possible. Thank You for being the source of my strength and inspiration.

To my grandmothers, thank you for laying the foundation of faith in my life. Your prayers and devotion to God continue to guide me. To my father, now in heaven, your love and lessons still inspire me, and I know you are watching over me with pride.

To my mother, Mabeline, thank you for your unwavering support and the values you instilled in me. To my siblings, Tia, Tamika, and Ray, your love and encouragement mean the world to me. To my nieces and nephews, you are a constant reminder of God's blessings—I hope this book inspires you as much as you inspire me.

To my client, whose story inspired this book—you know who you are. Your courage and honesty are a testament to God's grace, and I pray these pages uplift you and others like you.

To my pastors, Drs. Dee Dee and Michael Freeman, thank you for your leadership and faith-filled teachings. Your guidance has been instrumental in my spiritual growth and this project.

Finally, to you, the reader, thank you for letting this book be a part of your journey. My prayer is that these affirmations remind you of your worth, inspire you to live boldly, and help you see yourself as God does—perfect in His eyes.

With gratitude,
Terri McColl

Overview

Perfect in His Eyes is a faith-filled guide designed to empower and encourage teenage Christian girls—and anyone seeking to build their self-esteem through God's truth.

Organized as an A-to-Z collection of affirmations, each entry explores a unique aspect of who God says you are—loved, chosen, extraordinary, and so much more. Every affirmation is paired with biblical insights, therapeutic reflections, and practical exercises to help readers internalize these truths and live boldly in faith.

Through journaling prompts, reflective questions, and uplifting prayers, *Perfect in His Eyes* equips readers with tools to silence self-doubt, embrace their God-given uniqueness, and live a life of purpose and confidence. Whether navigating the challenges of adolescence, seeking personal growth, or encouraging someone else on their journey, this book serves as a reminder that you are fearfully and wonderfully made.

Key Features:

- A-to-Z affirmations grounded in Scripture
- Practical exercises for reflection and personal growth
- Uplifting prayers and journaling prompts
- Encouragement for readers of all ages

You are not defined by the opinions of others or by worldly measures of success. You are defined by the One who calls you His own. This book is a reminder that you are cherished, valued, and always *Perfect in His Eyes*.

Table of Contents

Foreword

The idea for *Perfect in His Eyes* came to life during a heartfelt therapy session with a teenage client who, despite having a wonderfully supportive family, struggled deeply with self-esteem. She couldn't see her worth or embrace the beauty and uniqueness that everyone else around her recognized. Her story was a reminder that even when we are surrounded by love, we can still wrestle with feelings of inadequacy and self-doubt.

This book was created for the teenager who feels unseen, the young woman searching for her identity, and anyone yearning to understand her worth. It's a reminder that your value is not based on what the world says about you but on the unwavering truth of who God says you are. You are fearfully and wonderfully made, created with intention, and deeply loved by your Creator.

Through faith-filled affirmations and biblical truths, *Perfect in His Eyes* is a guide to rediscovering your God-given identity. Each page speaks to the heart, offering encouragement and hope while challenging the lies of self-doubt. My prayer is that as you read these affirmations, you'll begin to see yourself through God's eyes—loved, chosen, and made perfect through Christ. Let this book remind you of your worth and inspire you to live boldly in the confidence of His promises.

Introduction

You are perfect just as you are—crafted with love, purpose, and care by the Creator of the universe. Yet, in a world filled with comparisons, criticism, and confusion, it's easy to lose sight of who you truly are. *Perfect in His Eyes: Faith-Filled Affirmations to Build Self-Esteem* is your guide to rediscovering the truth about yourself through the eyes of God.

This book is for anyone who has ever doubted her worth, struggled with self-confidence, or wondered if she was enough. Rooted in therapeutic insights and anchored in Christian principles, each chapter will take you on a journey through the alphabet, using powerful affirmations and Bible verses to remind you of the truth about who you are: loved, valued, and cherished.

Here, you'll explore what it means to embrace your God-given identity, overcome self-doubt, and walk in the confidence that you were made with divine purpose. Alongside inspiring words, you'll find reflective prompts, journaling exercises, and practical tools to help you apply these truths to your daily life.

As you turn each page, my prayer is that you will see yourself through God's eyes—fearfully and wonderfully made, full of potential, and capable of living a bold and beautiful life. This is more than just a book; it's a reminder of the truth that will set you free. So, grab a pen, open your heart, and let's begin this journey of discovering who you are: *perfect in His eyes!*

A -Amazing, Awesome & Adored

You are amazing—not because of what you achieve, how you look, or what others think about you—but because of who you are: a unique creation of the Almighty God. In a world that often tries to measure your worth by achievements or appearances, know this truth: God has already declared you more than enough.

When God designed you, He did so with intention and love. You are "fearfully and wonderfully made" (Psalm 139:14), not by accident but by divine craftsmanship. Take a moment to think about all the qualities that make you unique—your kindness, your smile, your ideas, and your dreams. These aren't random; they are gifts that God has planted within you for a purpose.

Sometimes, self-doubt and comparison can cloud the truth of your worth. Those feelings may stem from painful experiences or unkind words you've heard in the past. But remember, your worth isn't defined by others' opinions or even by your own feelings. It's defined by God's truth.

When you see yourself through God's eyes, you'll realize that you are adored, able, and filled with incredible potential. Your job isn't to prove your worth; it's to embrace the worth God has already given you.

Words to remember: Amazing, Awesome & Adored
Bible Verse: "I praise you because I am fearfully and wonderfully made; your works are wonderful. I know that full well."
Psalm 139:1

Reflect and Write

1. What does being "amazing" mean to you?
Write about moments in your life when you've felt amazing—not because of what you achieved, but because of who you are.

_____

_____

_____

_____

_____

_____

2. What unique gifts has God placed in you?
List three qualities or talents that make you special. Consider how you can use them to reflect God's love to others.

1._____
2._____
3._____

3. How can you use them to reflect God's love to others?

_____

_____

_____

3. How can you see yourself through God's eyes today?

Write down a situation where you've struggled with self-doubt. Then, rewrite that situation as if God is speaking encouragement to you.

_____
_____
_____
_____
_____
_____
_____
_____
_____
_____
_____
_____
_____
_____
_____
_____
_____
_____
_____
_____
_____

Seeing Yourself As Amazing

1. Words to Describe Me
Fill in the blanks with "A" words that affirm your worth:

- I am _____.
- I am _____.
- I am _____.

2. Mirror Exercise
Stand in front of a mirror and say the following:

- "I am amazing because God made me."
- "I am enough just as I am."
- "I am loved by God, always."

How did that exercise make you feel?

_____

_____

_____

_____

_____

_____

3. Prayer for the Day
Heavenly Father, thank You for making me amazing in Your image. Help me to see myself through Your eyes, to silence the doubts, and to walk confidently in the truth of who I am. Amen.

B - Brave, Bold & Beloved

You are brave, even when you feel afraid. Bravery isn't about never feeling fear; it's about trusting God to walk with you through the fear. In moments of doubt, remember that God has equipped you with strength and courage to face challenges. He promises to never leave you, even in your hardest moments.

When you feel overwhelmed, remind yourself that bravery isn't about being perfect—it's about showing up and trusting God to guide you. Whether it's standing up for what's right, trying something new, or overcoming a past hurt, your courage is a reflection of God's strength in you.

Words to Remember: Brave, Bold & Beloved
Bible Verse:
"Have I not commanded you? Be strong and courageous. Do not be afraid; do not be discouraged, for the Lord your God will be with you wherever you go." — Joshua 1:9

Reflect and Write

1.When have you shown bravery in the past?

Write about a moment when you stepped out of your comfort zone or overcame a fear.

_____

_____

_____

_____

_____

2. What fears are you facing right now?

List them, and then write a prayer asking God to give you courage.

_____

_____

_____

_____

_____

3. How can you practice bravery this week?

Write one small step you can take to face your fears with God's help.

_____

_____

_____

_____

𝒫racticing 𝒷ravery

1. Fear List: Write down three fears that hold you back.

1._____

2._____

3._____

2. God's Promise: For each fear, write how God's Word reassures you. Example: "I fear failure, but God says I can do all things through Christ who strengthens me."

Fear:_____

1._____

_____

_____

Fear:_____

2._____

_____

_____

Fear:_____

3._____

_____

_____

3. Action Plan: Choose one fear and write a step you can take to face it this week.
The fear is:

_____

_____

The step that I will take to face it this week:

_____

_____

_____

_____

_____

_____

Prayer for Bravery:
God, I feel afraid, but I trust that You are with me. Help me to be brave, to face my fears, and to remember that Your strength is greater than my worries. Amen.

Additional thoughts:

_____

_____

_____

_____

_____

C - Chosen, Cherished & Called

You are chosen by God for a purpose. You are not here by accident; God created you intentionally and uniquely for His glory. Being chosen means that you have value and worth, no matter what the world tells you.

God, in His infinite wisdom, looked at you and said, "I want you." Before you were even born, He formed you with a specific purpose in mind. You are a part of His grand design, and your life holds meaning beyond what you can imagine.

When you feel unseen or unimportant, remember that God sees you fully and knows your heart. He has set you apart as His beloved, and He cherishes every detail of who you are. You don't have to fight for a place in this world—you already belong to Him. The Creator of the universe has called you by name, and no one can take that away from you.

Being chosen by God also means that He equips you for the purpose He has for you. Even when you face challenges, He provides the strength, wisdom, and guidance you need to fulfill your destiny. You don't have to do it alone; His presence is with you every step of the way.

Words to Remember: Chosen, Cherished & Called
Bible Verse:
"You did not choose me, but I chose you and appointed you so that you might go and bear fruit—fruit that will last." — John 15:16

Reflect and Write

1.How does it feel to know you are chosen by God?
Write about what this truth means to you.

_____

_____

_____

_____

2.What gifts or talents has God chosen you to use?
List three ways you can use these to serve others and bring glory to God.

1._____

2. _____

3._____

3.Who reminds you of your worth in Christ?
Write about someone who encourages you to see yourself as chosen and loved.

_____

_____

_____

_____

_____

Living as Someone Chosen

1.Who Am I in Christ? Write a sentence beginning with, "I am chosen because..."

_____
_____
_____

2. Bearing Fruit: Write one way you can use your gifts to bless someone this week.

_____
_____
_____

3. Prayer of Purpose: Write a prayer asking God to guide you in fulfilling His purpose for your life.

_____
_____
_____
_____

Prayer for the Day:
God, thank You for choosing me and giving my life meaning. Help me to trust in Your plan and to live each day as a reflection of Your love. Amen.

𝒟 ~ 𝒟etermined, 𝒟isciplined & 𝒟evoted

You are determined, and that determination is a gift from God. Even when life feels hard, you have the strength to keep going because God is with you. He has equipped you with resilience to overcome obstacles.

Your determination reflects God's power in you. The same God who parted the Red Sea and strengthened David to face Goliath empowers you to stand firm. In moments when giving up seems easier, your determination becomes a testament to His faithfulness.

When the road feels overwhelming, remember: God's power is made perfect in your weakness. Trust His promises and look to the One who makes all things possible. Every time you press on, you declare that His plan is greater than your struggles.

Determination is not just about pushing forward; it's about trusting that God's plan is greater than the struggles you face. Let your determination be fueled by the knowledge that you are never alone and that the Creator of the universe is your greatest support.

Words to Remember: Determined, Disciplined & Devoted
Bible Verse:
"Blessed is the one who perseveres under trial because, having stood the test, that person will receive the crown of life that the Lord has promised to those who love him."
— James 1:12

Reflect and Write

1.What challenges are you currently facing?
Write about an area in your life where you need determination.

_____
_____
_____
_____
_____

2.When have you overcome a trial in the past?
Reflect on how God helped you through it.

_____
_____
_____
_____
_____

3.What motivates you to stay determined?
Write about a goal or promise from God that inspires you to keep going.

_____
_____
_____
_____
_____

Staying Determined

1.Challenge List: Write one challenge you are facing and a bible verse that encourages you.

_____
_____
_____
_____

2.God's Strength: Reflect on how God has helped you persevere in the past.

_____
_____
_____
_____

Prayer of Determination: Write a prayer asking God for strength to stay determined.

_____
_____
_____

Prayer for the Day:
Lord, help me to stay determined even when life feels hard. Remind me that You are my strength and that I can do all things through You. Amen.

Additional thoughts:

_____
_____
_____

E – Empowered, Equipped & Encouraged

You are empowered because God's Spirit lives within you. He has given you everything you need to face life's challenges with confidence. You are not weak or helpless—you are equipped with strength, wisdom, and love to overcome any obstacle. You are encouraged by His promises, which remind you that you are never alone and that He is always working on your behalf.

Being empowered means walking in the authority that God has given you, knowing that His power works in you and through you. It's understanding that you have been chosen, called, and equipped for a purpose greater than yourself. You don't have to rely solely on your strength because God's grace is sufficient for every situation.

When fear or doubt tries to hold you back, remember that you are a vessel of God's power. He has entrusted you with unique gifts and abilities, and He will guide you as you use them to glorify Him. Step forward with courage, knowing that God has already equipped you for the path He has called you to walk. His Spirit encourages you daily, reminding you that you are more than a conqueror through Him who loves you.

Words to Remember: Empowered, Equipped & Encouraged
Bible Verse:
"For the Spirit God gave us does not make us timid, but gives us power, love, and self-discipline." — 2 Timothy 1:7

Reflect and Write

1.What makes you feel empowered?
Write about a time when you felt strong and capable.

_____
_____
_____
_____

2. What challenges make you feel powerless?
Reflect on these situations and write a prayer asking God for His strength.

_____
_____
_____
_____

3. How can you use God's power to help someone else?
Write one way you can empower someone this week.

_____
_____
_____
_____

Living Empowered

1.I Am Empowered: Write a sentence starting with, "I am empowered because..."

_____

_____

_____

2. Power in Action: Think of one area where you feel stuck. Write a step you can take, knowing God's Spirit is with you.

_____

_____

_____

3. Encouraging Others: Write a kind word or action you can do to encourage someone else today.

_____

_____

_____

Prayer for the Day:
Lord, thank You for empowering me with Your Spirit. Help me to walk boldly in Your love and share that strength with others. Amen.

F ~ Faithful, Focused & Fruitful

Your faithfulness is a reflection of your trust in Him and your commitment to live according to His Word. It's not about being perfect; it's about staying devoted to God even when life feels hard, uncertain, or overwhelming. Faithfulness is choosing to believe in His goodness and promises, even in moments when you can't yet see the outcome.

Being faithful means showing up with a willing heart, doing your best, and trusting God to handle the rest. It means staying consistent in prayer, holding onto hope when doubt creeps in, and leaning on His strength when yours feels weak. Your faithfulness honors God, strengthens your relationship with Him, and builds your character in ways that prepare you for greater blessings.

Remember, God treasures your faithfulness, no matter how small it may seem to you. Each act of devotion— whether it's offering a kind word, standing firm in your values, or simply trusting Him in the silence—is seen and celebrated by Him. Your faithfulness is a testimony of His work in your life, and through it, you inspire others to trust in His unchanging love.

Words to Remember: Faithful, Focused & Fruitful
Bible Verse:
"Let love and faithfulness never leave you; bind them around your neck, write them on the tablet of your heart." — Proverbs 3:3

Reflect and Write

1.What does faithfulness mean to you?
Reflect on a time when you stayed committed to something important.

_____

_____

_____

_____

2.How do you see God's faithfulness in your life?
Write about a time when God came through for you.

_____

_____

_____

_____

3.What helps you stay faithful to God?
Write one practice that strengthens your faith (e.g., prayer, Bible reading).

_____

_____

_____

_____

Strengthening Faithfulness

1.Faithfulness Reflection: Write, "I can be faithful because God is faithful to me."

_____

_____

2. Daily Devotion: List one small way you can show faithfulness to God today (e.g., pray before a meal).

_____

_____

3. Encouraging Faithfulness in Others: Write about someone whose faithfulness inspires you.

_____

_____

Prayer for the Day:
God, thank You for Your faithfulness to me. Help me to stay devoted to You in all areas of my life. Amen.

Additional thoughts:

_____

_____

_____

G – Grateful, Giving & Graceful

You are grateful because God has filled your life with blessings, both big and small. Gratitude shifts your focus from what you lack to what you have, reminding you of His abundant love and provision. It helps you see that even in life's hardest moments, His grace is present, working for your good.

Gratitude is not about ignoring your challenges; instead, it's about choosing to see God's goodness through them. It's in the simple joys—a kind word, a sunrise, or the strength to face another day—that God reveals His care. When you cultivate a heart of gratitude, you invite joy and peace into your life, and you strengthen your trust in God's faithfulness.

Even in seasons of waiting or difficulty, there's always something to be thankful for. A grateful heart aligns you with God's perspective, allowing you to see His hand at work in ways you might otherwise overlook. By practicing gratitude, you declare that God is enough and that His blessings are more than sufficient for you.

Words to Remember: Grateful, Giving & Graceful
Bible Verse:
"Give thanks in all circumstances; for this is God's will for you in Christ Jesus." — 1 Thessalonians 5:18

Reflect and Write

1.What are you grateful for today?
Write down three things that make you feel thankful.

1._____
2._____
3._____

2. How does gratitude help you feel closer to God?
Reflect on how giving thanks changes your perspective.

_____

_____

_____

3. Who has blessed your life recently?
Write about someone you're thankful for and how you can show them your appreciation.

_____

_____

_____

Practicing Gratitude

1.Gratitude List: Write three things you are thankful for every day this week.

Sunday_____
Monday_____
Tuesday_____
Wednesday_____
Thursday_____
Friday_____
Saturday_____

2. Blessing Others: Think of someone who has blessed you. Write a kind note or text to thank them.
Person who has blessed me:_____

3. God's Grace: Write a short prayer thanking God for one specific blessing in your life.

_____
_____
_____

Prayer for the Day:
Lord, thank You for the many blessings in my life. Help me to have a heart full of gratitude and to share Your goodness with others. Amen.

H ~ Hopeful, Healed & Happy

You are hopeful because God's plans for you are good and full of promise. No matter what challenges you face, hope reminds you that better days are ahead, grounded in God's love and faithfulness. Hope is not wishful thinking; it's the anchor that steadies your soul, even in life's storms. It whispers to your heart that God's grace is greater than any difficulty you encounter.

Being hopeful means trusting that God is working everything out for your good, even when the path is unclear. It's not about ignoring the hard times but choosing to focus on the possibilities and promises that God has for your future. With hope, you can navigate life's challenges with courage, knowing that His plans for you are greater than anything you could imagine.

Hope fuels your perseverance and ignites your faith. When you feel weary, lean into God's promises, for He is the ultimate source of hope. Your hopeful spirit is a light to those around you, a reminder that God's goodness is ever-present and His love never fails.

Words to Remember: Hopeful, Healed & Happy
Bible Verse:
"For I know the plans I have for you," declares the Lord, "plans to prosper you and not to harm you, plans to give you hope and a future." — Jeremiah 29:11

Reflect and Write

1.What are you hopeful for?
Write about one dream or goal that gives you hope.

_____
_____
_____
_____

2. When has God restored your hope in the past?
Reflect on a time when something good came out of a difficult situation.

_____
_____
_____
_____

3.How can you share hope with someone else?
Think of one way to encourage someone who may be struggling.

_____
_____
_____

Holding Onto Hope

1.Hope Reminder: Write, "I am hopeful because God is with me, and He has great plans for my life."

_____

_____

2. Future Vision: Draw or write about a picture of your life five years from now—filled with the blessings you're hoping for.

_____
_____
_____
_____
_____

3. Encouragement Note: Write an encouraging message to someone who might need hope.

_____
_____
_____
_____

Prayer for the Day:
God, thank You for being my source of hope. Help me to trust in Your promises and share hope with others. Amen.

I – Inspired, Intentional & Invincible

You are inspired because God has placed unique dreams and passions in your heart, intricately woven into your being by His divine purpose. You are fearfully and wonderfully made, created to do amazing things that reflect His glory. His Spirit empowers you, giving you strength, wisdom, and courage to live a life of purpose that impacts others.

Inspiration comes from within, ignited by your faith and nurtured by the unique talents and gifts God has given you. It is a spark that grows as you align your heart with His will and trust His plans for your life. Being inspired means looking to God as your ultimate guide, drawing strength and encouragement from His Word, which is a lamp unto your feet and a light unto your path.

It also means believing wholeheartedly in the possibilities He has laid before you, even when the journey feels uncertain. Inspiration propels you to dream boldly, to step out in faith, and to pursue your goals with unwavering confidence. It is a reminder that with God, all things are possible, and He will equip you for every good work He calls you to do.

Words to Remember: Inspired, Intentional & Invincible
Bible Verse:
"But those who hope in the Lord will renew their strength. They will soar on wings like eagles; they will run and not grow weary, they will walk and not be faint." — Isaiah 40:31

Reflect and Write

1.What inspires you?
Write about what lights up your heart and brings you joy.

_____
_____
_____
_____

2. How can God's Word inspire you?
Reflect on a Bible verse or story that motivates you to keep going.

_____
_____
_____
_____

3. What steps can you take toward your dreams?
Write one action you can take this week to move closer to your goals.

_____
_____
_____
_____

Living an Inspired Life

1.Daily Inspiration: Write, "I am inspired because God has a purpose for my life."

_____
_____
_____

2. Dream Board: Create a small vision board (draw or write) with images or words that inspire you.

_____
_____
_____

3. Inspire Others: Write a motivational note or message to share with a friend.

_____
_____
_____

Prayer for the Day:
Lord, thank You for inspiring me to live with purpose. Help me to pursue the dreams You've placed in my heart and to inspire others along the way. Amen.

J ~ Joyful, Jubilant & Justified

You are joyful because God fills your life with His boundless love and unshakable peace. Joy is more than a fleeting emotion that comes and goes with circumstances; it is a deep, abiding sense of contentment and hope, rooted in the knowledge that God walks with you through every season of life. His presence transforms even the hardest moments into opportunities for growth and renewal, allowing joy to spring forth like a well in the desert.

Being joyful doesn't mean life is always easy or that you're happy all the time. It means making a conscious decision to trust in God's promises, even when the weight of the world feels heavy. Joy comes from knowing that He is in control, that His plans for you are good, and that nothing can separate you from His love. It is found in the quiet, beautiful moments—a sunrise, a kind word, a prayer answered in an unexpected way—and in the deep assurance that God's grace is sufficient for every need.

Your joy is not only a gift to you but also a blessing to those around you. It is contagious, spreading light and hope in a world often filled with darkness. When you live with joy, you reflect God's Spirit within you, reminding others that His love is greater than any challenge they face. Let His joy fill your heart, strengthening you for the journey ahead, and radiating as a beacon of faith to all who encounter you. Truly, the joy of the Lord is your strength.

Words to Remember: Joyful, Jubilant & Justified
Bible Verse:
"The joy of the Lord is your strength." — Nehemiah 8:10

Reflect and Write

1.What brings you joy?
List three things that fill your heart with happiness.

1._____
2._____
3._____

2. How does God's love bring you joy?
Reflect on His promises and write how they give you strength.

_____
_____
_____
_____

3. How can you share joy with someone else?
Write about a small act of kindness you can do today to brighten someone's day.

_____
_____
_____
_____
_____

Cultivating Joy

1.Joy Journal: Write, "I am joyful because God's love fills my heart."

_____

_____

_____

2. Gratitude List: List three blessings from today that make you smile.

1._____

2._____

3._____

3. Spread Joy: Plan one simple way to bring joy to someone this week, like a smile, a compliment, or a small gift.

_____

_____

_____

_____

Prayer for the Day:
God, thank You for filling my heart with joy. Help me to share this joy with others and to trust in Your goodness every day. Amen.

K ~ Kind, Kept & Known

You are kind because God's love flows through you, a reflection of His character and grace. Kindness is more than an action—it's a way to make His love visible in a world that longs for compassion. Every kind word and gesture carries the power to reflect His goodness and remind others that they are loved and valued.

Being kind doesn't mean pleasing everyone; it means choosing respect, compassion, and understanding, even when it's challenging. It is a strength that comes from knowing you are deeply loved by God, enabling you to love others freely without expecting anything in return.

Your kindness has the power to inspire hope, heal hearts, and change lives—including your own. When you act with kindness, you are spreading God's light and helping to make the world a better place. Let your kindness reflect the love He has poured into you, showing His grace in every interaction.

As you walk in kindness, you are living out His purpose for your life, becoming a beacon of His peace and love. Let your kindness be a daily offering that honors Him and draws others toward His unfailing grace.

Words to Remember: Kind, Kept & Known
Bible Verse:
"Be kind and compassionate to one another, forgiving each other, just as in Christ God forgave you." — Ephesians 4:32

Reflect and Write

1.How do you show kindness to others?
Reflect on ways you've shared kindness recently.

_____
_____
_____
_____
_____

2. When have you experienced unexpected kindness?
Write about how it impacted your heart.

_____
_____
_____
_____
_____

3. Who could use a little kindness today?
List one act of kindness you can do for them.

_____
_____
_____
_____
_____

Sharing Kindness

1.Daily Reminder: Write, "I am kind because God's love flows through me."

_____

_____

_____

2. Kindness Plan: Think of one person you can bless today and write how you will do it.

_____

_____

_____

3. Gratitude Reflection: Write about a time someone was kind to you and how it made you feel.

_____

_____

_____

_____

Prayer for the Day:
God, thank You for Your kindness toward me. Help me to share that kindness with others and to be a light in their lives. Amen.

ℒ ~ Loved, Loved & Light

You are loved deeply and unconditionally by God. His love is not earned through your actions, achievements, or perfection—it flows freely from who He is: a God of grace, mercy, and compassion. You are cherished beyond measure, and nothing—no mistake, failure, or hardship—can ever separate you from His boundless love.

When you feel unworthy, unloved, or forgotten, hold tightly to the truth that God's love is constant and unchanging. He sees you completely—your flaws, fears, strengths, and dreams—and still chooses to love you with an everlasting, unwavering love. His love is not conditional on who you are but on who He is.

Being loved by God gives you the freedom to love yourself, embracing who He created you to be, and the strength to extend that love to others. It is a foundation that provides security and hope, reminding you that no matter what challenges or uncertainties you face, you are never alone. His love surrounds you, carries you, and sustains you through every high and low.

Let His love be your light in times of darkness, your peace in moments of doubt, and your joy in every season of life.

Words to Remember: Loved, Lovable & Light
Bible Verse:
"And so we know and rely on the love God has for us. God is love. Whoever lives in love lives in God, and God in them." — 1 John 4:16

Reflect and Write

1.How does knowing you are loved by God change how you see yourself?
Reflect on how His love has shaped your identity.

_____

_____

_____

_____

2. When do you feel closest to God's love?
Write about moments that remind you of His presence.

_____

_____

_____

_____

3. How can you show love to yourself today?
List one way to care for yourself as God's cherished creation.

_____

_____

_____

_____

Resting in Love

1.Daily Affirmation: Write, "I am loved unconditionally by God."

_____
_____
_____

2. Love Reminder: Write a note to yourself, starting with "Dear [Your Name], You are loved because…"

_____
_____
_____
_____

3. Gratitude Exercise: List three things that remind you of God's love today.

1._____
2._____
3._____

Prayer for the Day:
Lord, thank You for loving me so deeply and completely. Help me to rest in Your love and share it with those around me. Amen.

P – Perfect, Peaceful & Purposeful

You are perfect in God's eyes, not because of what you do but because of who you are in Christ. Through His sacrifice, He has made you holy, blameless, and righteous.

The world may tell you that perfection is unattainable, but God sees you as His masterpiece, created in His image and for His glory. When you feel unworthy or flawed, remember that His grace covers you, and His love perfects you. You don't have to strive to earn His approval—you already have it.

Being perfect in Christ allows you to walk in confidence and peace. You can let go of the pressure to meet worldly standards and instead rest in the truth of who God says you are. His perfection working in you empowers you to live a life of purpose and joy.

Embrace the freedom of being made perfect through Christ. Let this truth transform how you see yourself and how you approach life. Your identity is not rooted in your imperfections but in God's perfect love and His work in you

Words to Remember: Perfect, Peaceful & Purposeful
Bible Verse:
"But He said to me, 'My grace is sufficient for you, for my power is made perfect in weakness.' Therefore, I will boast all the more gladly about my weaknesses, so that Christ's power may rest on me." — 2 Corinthians 12:9

Reflect and Write

1.What does perfection in Christ mean to you?
Reflect on how His love makes you whole, even when you feel incomplete.

_____

_____

_____

_____

2. When have you experienced God's grace in your life?
Write about a time when His grace gave you strength.

_____

_____

_____

_____

3. What would you say to someone who feels they are not enough?
Write a letter of encouragement, reminding them of God's perfect love.

_____

_____

_____

_____

1. Daily Affirmation: Write, "I am perfect because Christ's love completes me."

_____

_____

2. Grace List: Reflect on three ways God's grace has carried you through difficult moments.

1._____

2._____

3._____

3. Graceful Acts: List one small way you can extend grace to yourself or someone else this week.

_____

_____

_____

Prayer for the Day:
Lord, thank You for making me perfect in Your love. Help me to let go of the need to strive for human perfection and rest in the truth that Your grace is sufficient for me. Amen.

Q ~ Quiet, Qualified & Quenched

You are qualified because God has called you and equipped you for His purpose. The world may question your abilities, but God has already given you everything you need to fulfill His plans. He doesn't call the qualified— He qualifies the called.

When feelings of inadequacy creep in, remind yourself that God's strength is made perfect in your weakness. You don't have to rely on your own skills or knowledge because His Spirit works through you, empowering you to do far more than you could on your own.

Your qualifications come from God's grace, not from your achievements. He sees your potential and uses even your past mistakes for His glory. Trust that His plans for you are good and that He will equip you for every step of the journey.

Walk boldly in the truth that you are qualified by God. Let this knowledge give you the confidence to step into new opportunities, embrace challenges, and fulfill the purpose He has placed on your life. You are capable, prepared, and chosen for greatness.

Words to Remember: Quiet, Qualified & Quenched
Bible Verse:
"In quietness and trust is your strength." — Isaiah 30:15

Reflect and Write

1.What do you hear when you take time to be quiet before God?
Reflect on what His voice brings to your heart.

_____
_____
_____
_____

2. How does being quiet strengthen you?
Write about a time when quietness helped you find peace.

_____
_____
_____
_____

3. What distractions can you let go of to embrace quiet moments?
Create a plan for moments of stillness in your day.

_____
_____
_____
_____

Finding Strength in Quiet

1.Daily Affirmation: Write, "I find strength in quiet moments with God."

_____

_____

_____

2. Quiet Reflection: Spend five minutes in silence with God and write what comes to mind.

_____

_____

_____

_____

3. Peace Plan: Write one way you can create a quiet space in your day.

_____

_____

_____

_____

Prayer for the Day:
Lord, help me to embrace the quiet and trust You in those moments. Renew my strength as I find peace in Your presence. Amen.

$\mathcal{R}$ ~ Redeemed, Restored & Radiant

You are redeemed by the love and sacrifice of Jesus Christ. Through His death and resurrection, He has bought you back from sin and made you new. Redemption means that your past no longer defines you—you are free to live in the fullness of God's grace.

Being redeemed means knowing that you are deeply loved and valued. God saw your worth even before you knew Him, and He paid the ultimate price to bring you into His family. When you feel weighed down by shame or regret, remember that His forgiveness has set you free.

Your redemption is a gift, not something you earn. It's a reminder of God's unchanging love and His ability to transform anything for good. Because you are redeemed, you can walk in freedom, joy, and peace, knowing that you belong to God.

Let your life reflect the beauty of redemption. Share your story of God's grace, and let others see the hope and transformation He has brought to your life. You are redeemed, restored, and made new by His unfailing love.

Words to Remember: Redeemed, Restored & Radiant
Bible Verse:
"In Him we have redemption through His blood, the forgiveness of sins, in accordance with the riches of God's grace." — Ephesians 1:7

Reflect and Write

1.What does redemption mean to you?
Write about how God's grace has changed your life.

_____
_____
_____
_____

2. How can you let go of your past and embrace your redeemed identity?
Reflect on what holds you back from fully accepting His grace.

_____
_____
_____
_____

3. What would you say to someone who feels unworthy of redemption?
Write a letter of encouragement to remind them of God's love.

_____
_____
_____
_____

Living as Redeemed

1.Daily Affirmation: Write, "I am redeemed and made whole by God's grace."

_____
_____
_____

2. Freedom List: Write three things from your past that God has redeemed.
1._____
2._____
3._____

3. Grace Exercise: Reflect on how you can extend grace to yourself today.

_____
_____
_____
_____

Prayer for the Day:
Lord, thank You for redeeming me and restoring my life. Help me to walk in the freedom of Your grace. Amen.

S ~ Strong, Secure & Saved

You are strong because God is your source of strength. Life's challenges may feel overwhelming, but His power sustains you and enables you to keep going. Your strength doesn't come from your circumstances but from your faith in the One who holds all things together.

God's Word reminds you that you can do all things through Christ who strengthens you. This strength is not just physical—it's emotional, mental, and spiritual. It equips you to face adversity, stand firm in your faith, and love others even when it's hard.

Being strong doesn't mean you never feel weak. It means that in your moments of weakness, you rely on God's strength to carry you through. His power is limitless, and He delights in giving you what you need to overcome life's challenges.

Embrace the strength God has given you, and let it be a light to others. When you walk in His strength, you are a testimony to His faithfulness and power. You are strong because He is strong in you.

Words to Remember: Strong, Secure & Saved
Bible Verse:
"The Lord is my strength and my shield; my heart trusts in Him, and He helps me." — Psalm 28:7

Reflect and Write

1.What does it mean to rely on God's strength?
Reflect on a time when His strength carried you.

_____
_____
_____
_____
_____

2. How can you remind yourself of your strength in Christ?
Write 3 affirmations or verses that inspire you.
1._____
2._____
3._____

3. When have you felt strongest in your faith?
Reflect on moments when you leaned on God and overcame challenges.

_____
_____
_____
_____
_____

Building Strength in Christ

1.Daily Affirmation: Write, "I am strong because God is my strength."

_____
_____
_____

2. Strength Journal: Write three challenges God has helped you overcome.

1._____
2._____
3._____

3. Action Plan: Identify one area in your life where you need God's strength today.

_____
_____
_____
_____
_____

Prayer for the Day:
Lord, thank You for being my strength. Help me to rely on You and trust Your power in my life. Amen.

T ~ Trustworthy, True & Tenacious

You are trustworthy because God has instilled in you a spirit of integrity and truth. Trust begins with honesty—with yourself, with others, and with God. It grows when you consistently align your actions with your words and reflect His character in your daily life. By seeking His guidance, you become a person others can depend on, someone whose actions inspire confidence and respect.

Being trustworthy is also about trusting in God's perfect plan for your life. When you place your faith in Him, you gain the strength to live authentically and honorably, even in uncertain times. Trusting God allows you to walk in obedience, knowing He is working all things for your good. This faith gives you the courage to stand firm in your values and remain steadfast in your commitments, even when faced with challenges.

Trustworthiness is a reflection of God's faithfulness to you. It is built through consistency, reliability, and a genuine commitment to doing what is right. Let your trust in God shape your character, empowering you to live with integrity and grace. As you grow in faith and trustworthiness, you inspire others to see the goodness of God through your life.

Words to Remember: Trustworthy, True, Tenacious
Bible Verse:
"Trust in the Lord with all your heart and lean not on your own understanding." — Proverbs 3:5

Reflect and Write

1.What does being trustworthy mean to you?
Reflect on how you show that you are worthy of trust to the people in your life.

_____

_____

_____

_____

2. How do you build trust in your relationship with God?
Write about ways you can deepen your faith.

_____

_____

_____

_____

3. Who inspires trust in your life?
Reflect on someone you admire for their honesty and faithfulness.

_____

_____

_____

_____

Living with Trust

1.Daily Affirmation: Write, "I am trustworthy and live with integrity."

_____

_____

2. Trust List: Write three ways you can build trust in your relationships.
1._____
2._____
3._____

3. Faith Reflection: Spend time in prayer, asking God to strengthen your trust in Him.

_____

_____

_____

_____

Prayer for the Day:
Lord, help me to be a trustworthy person and to trust in Your perfect plan for my life. Amen.

Additional Thoughts:

_____

_____

U - Unstoppable, Unique & Uplifted

You are unstoppable when you walk in faith, trusting God to guide your steps. With Him by your side, no obstacle is too great, and no challenge is too overwhelming. The same power that created the heavens and the earth is working within you, giving you the strength and determination to keep moving forward.

Being unstoppable doesn't mean life will be free of difficulties. Challenges will come, and setbacks may test your resolve, but they cannot hold you back when your foundation is in God. Perseverance flows from the deep assurance that His power is far greater than anything you face. Even in moments of doubt or weakness, His grace is sufficient, and His strength is made perfect in your limitations.

Walking in faith makes you resilient. It allows you to press on through fear, uncertainty, and hardship, knowing that God's plan for your life is good. Being unstoppable is not about never falling—it's about rising every time, knowing that God will lift you up and lead you onward.

Let your unstoppable spirit be a reflection of God's power within you. Trust His timing, embrace His guidance, and boldly pursue the path He has laid before you.

Words to Remember: Unstoppable, Unique & Uplifted
Bible Verse:
"I can do all things through Christ who strengthens me."
— Philippians 4:13

Reflect and Write

1.What does being unstoppable mean to you?
Reflect on how God gives you strength to keep going.

_____
_____
_____

2. What challenges have you overcome by trusting in God?
Write about a time when you didn't give up, even when it was hard.

_____
_____
_____
_____

3. How can you encourage others to be unstoppable in their faith?
Write a message of encouragement for someone who feels stuck.

_____
_____
_____
_____

Walking in Faith

1.Daily Affirmation: Write, "I am unstoppable because God strengthens me."

_____
_____
_____

2. Perseverance Plan: Write down one challenge you are facing and how you'll trust God to overcome it.

_____
_____
_____

3. Action Step: Identify one step you can take today to move closer to your goal.

_____
_____
_____

Prayer for the Day:
Lord, thank You for making me unstoppable through Your strength. Help me to persevere and trust You in all things. Amen.

V – Victorious, Valued & Vibrant

You are victorious because Jesus has already won the ultimate battle for you. On the cross, He defeated sin, death, and every power that could ever stand against you. Through Him, you are more than a conqueror, equipped with the strength, wisdom, and grace to overcome anything life brings your way.

Victory in Christ means that you don't have to fight life's battles on your own. You are not striving in your own strength, but resting in His. When challenges arise, trust in Him to be your defender and guide.

Being victorious doesn't mean life will always be easy, but it does mean that every trial you face is an opportunity to see God's hand at work. He transforms your struggles into testimonies of His goodness and uses even your setbacks to lead you into greater purpose.

Let your victory in Christ fill you with hope and confidence. You are already standing on the winning side because He has gone before you, ensuring that no weapon formed against you will prosper. Trust in His plan, lean into His strength, and celebrate the truth that in every season, you are victorious through Him

Words to Remember: Victorious, Valued & Vibrant
Bible Verse:
"But thanks be to God! He gives us the victory through our Lord Jesus Christ." — 1 Corinthians 15:57

Reflect and Write

1.What does victory in Christ mean to you?
Reflect on how His power has worked in your life.

_____

_____

_____

2. How can you celebrate the victories God has given you?
Write about a recent win, no matter how small, and thank God for it.

_____

_____

_____

_____

_____

3. What battles are you trusting God to fight for you?
Reflect on areas where you need His help.

_____

_____

_____

_____

_____

Living Victoriously

1.Daily Affirmation: Write, "I am victorious through Christ."

_____
_____
_____

2. Victory List: Write three ways God has helped you overcome challenges.
1._____
2._____
3._____

3. Thanksgiving Exercise: Spend time in prayer, thanking God for the victories in your life.

_____
_____
_____
_____

Prayer for the Day:
Lord, thank You for making me victorious in You. Help me to trust in Your strength and celebrate the triumphs You bring. Amen.

W - Worthy, Wise, Wonderful

You are worthy, not because of what you've done or achieved, but because of who God says you are. You are His beloved child, chosen and cherished beyond measure. Your worth is not tied to worldly standards, accomplishments, or the opinions of others—it is anchored in the unchanging truth of God's love for you. He created you with purpose, beauty, and value that nothing and no one can diminish.

When self-doubt or insecurity creeps in, remember that your worth is not something you have to earn. It is a gift from God, freely given and rooted in His grace. He sees you fully, knowing your flaws, fears, and imperfections, and still calls you worthy of His love, respect, and blessings. Nothing you do—no success or failure—can add to or take away from the worth He has already placed on your life.

Embracing your worth means accepting His truth and rejecting the lies that tell you otherwise. It means walking confidently in His promises, knowing that you are fearfully and wonderfully made. As you rest in the assurance of His love, let it shape how you see yourself and how you interact with the world.

Words to Remember: Worthy, Wise & Wonderful
Bible Verse:
"You are precious and honored in my sight, and I love you." — Isaiah 43:4

Reflect and Write

1.What does it mean to know your worth in Christ?

Reflect on how God sees you.

_____

_____

_____

_____

2.How can you remind yourself of your worth when you feel unworthy?

Write about affirmations or Bible verses that inspire you.

_____

_____

_____

_____

3. How does knowing your worth help you treat others with love and kindness?

Reflect on how God's love shapes your actions.

_____

_____

_____

_____

Embracing Your Worth

1.Daily Affirmation: Write, "I am worthy because God loves me."

_____
_____
_____

2. Self-Worth List: Write three qualities you love about yourself.

1._____
2._____
3._____

3. Kindness Plan: Identify one way you can show love to yourself today.

_____
_____
_____
_____
_____

Prayer for the Day:
Lord, thank You for making me worthy in Your eyes. Help me to embrace my worth and reflect Your love to others. Amen.

X - Extraordinary, Excellent & Exemplary

You are extraordinary because God created you with unique gifts, talents, and a purpose that only you can fulfill. God designed every part of you intentionally, weaving together your strengths, passions, and even your quirks to reflect His glory.

Being extraordinary doesn't mean striving for perfection or comparing yourself to others. It means embracing your God-given uniqueness and living boldly in the purpose He has for you. You don't have to fit into anyone else's mold or meet the world's expectations. God has called you to be exactly who you are, and that is more than enough.

Living as the extraordinary person God made you to be requires courage, faith, and trust in His plan. It means stepping into your gifts with confidence, even when the path feels uncertain. When you embrace who you are in Him, you inspire others to do the same, showing the world what it looks like to live authentically and purposefully.

Remember that your extraordinary nature is not defined by what you do but by who you are in Christ. Let His light shine through you, illuminating the beauty and uniqueness He has placed within you.

Words to Remember: Extraordinary, Excellent & Exemplary
Bible Verse:
"Now to Him who is able to do immeasurably more than all we ask or imagine, according to His power that is at work within us." — Ephesians 3:20

Reflect and Write

1.What makes you extraordinary?
Write about your unique gifts and talents.

_____
_____
_____
_____
_____

2. How can you use your gifts to glorify God?
Reflect on ways you can serve others.

_____
_____
_____
_____
_____

3. What does it mean to live boldly in your faith?
Write about how you can step into your purpose.

_____
_____
_____
_____
_____

Living Extraordinary

1.Daily Affirmation: Write, "I am extraordinary because God created me uniquely."

_____
_____
_____

2. Gift List: Write down three talents or qualities that make you special.
1._____
2._____
3._____

3. Bold Action: Identify one way you will step into your God-given purpose today.

_____
_____
_____
_____

Prayer for the Day:
Lord, thank You for making me extraordinary. Help me to live boldly and use my gifts for Your glory. Amen.

Y - Youthful, Yearning & Yielding

You are youthful in spirit, embracing the joy and energy that comes from walking with God. Youthfulness isn't defined by age but by a heart that is alive with hope, curiosity, and faith. In Christ, you are renewed each day, empowered to live boldly and with purpose. His presence fills you with joy and the strength to approach life with enthusiasm, no matter the challenges you face.

When you embrace your youthful spirit, you reflect God's love and vibrancy in every aspect of your life. It means trusting Him like a child trusts a loving parent, knowing He will guide and protect you. This youthful faith keeps your heart open to His promises and helps you find joy in both the simple and profound moments of life.

Let your youthful spirit be a light to others, showing them the beauty of a life rooted in God's love. By leaning into His Word, worshiping with gratitude, and living with purpose, you inspire those around you to approach life with the same joy and passion. Through God's strength, you can rise above challenges and continue to shine as a reflection of His glory.

Words to Remember: Youthful, Yearning & Yielding
Bible Verse:
"He renews my strength. He guides me along right paths, bringing honor to His name." — Psalm 23:3

Reflect and Write

1.What does being youthful in spirit mean to you?

_____

_____

_____

_____

_____

2. How can you embrace a youthful mindset in your daily life?

_____

_____

_____

_____

_____

3. What steps can you take to find joy in God's presence every day?

_____

_____

_____

_____

Living Youthful

1.Daily Affirmation: Write, "I am youthful in spirit, renewed by God's love."

_____
_____
_____

2. Joy Journal: List three things that bring you joy and remind you of God's goodness.

1._____
2,_____
3._____

3. Faith Exercise: Spend five minutes in gratitude, thanking God for the ways He renews your strength and fills your life with purpose.

_____
_____
_____
_____

Prayer for the Day:
Lord, renew my spirit and fill my heart with Your joy and strength. Help me to live with youthful faith, trusting You in every step I take. Amen.

Z - Zealous, Zestful and Zany

You are zealous for God's love, boldly living out your faith with passion and purpose. Your zeal is a reflection of your gratitude for His unending grace and a response to His deep love for you. It is the fire in your heart that drives you to seek Him wholeheartedly and to follow His will, even when the path feels uncertain. This passion sets you apart, giving you strength and courage to stand firm in your faith.

Being zealous doesn't mean being perfect or never facing challenges. It means being fully committed to growing in your relationship with God and trusting Him through every season of life. Your zeal is about pursuing Him with a willing heart, aligning your life with His Word, and embracing the unique purpose He has for you. This dedication not only strengthens your faith but also encourages others to see the beauty of living for Him.

Let your zeal be a light that shines brightly in the world. Through prayer, worship, and staying grounded in His Word, your passion will continue to grow and inspire those around you. Trust that God will use your zeal to impact lives, fulfill His plans for you, and bring glory to His name. In your zeal, you become a reflection of His love and a reminder of the joy and hope found in Him.

Words to Remember: Zealous, Zestful & Zany
Bible Verse:
"Never be lacking in zeal, but keep your spiritual fervor, serving the Lord." — Romans 12:11

Reflect and Write

1. What does zeal for God look like in your life?
Write about ways you show your love for Him.

_____

_____

_____

_____

_____

2. How can you keep your passion for God alive?
Reflect on ways to stay connected to Him daily.

_____

_____

_____

_____

_____

3. Who inspires you with their zeal for God?
Write about someone whose faith motivates you.

_____

_____

_____

_____

_____

Living with Passion

1.Daily Affirmation: Write, "I am zealous for God's love and purpose."

_____
_____
_____

2.Passion Plan: Write one way you can serve God passionately this week.

_____
_____
_____
_____

3.Gratitude Exercise: Reflect on how God's love fuels your faith and enthusiasm.

_____
_____
_____
_____

Prayer for the Day:
Lord, thank You for giving me a zealous heart.
Help me to live boldly and inspire others with my faith.
Amen.

Final Thoughts

As you reach the end of *Perfect in His Eyes*, remember that this is not the end of your story—it's the beginning of living fully in the truth of who you are in Christ. Through these affirmations, you've been reminded of your identity: loved, chosen, purposeful, extraordinary, and made perfect in Him. These truths are not fleeting ideas; they are the foundation of who you are in the eyes of your Creator, who sees you as fearfully and wonderfully made.

You are made perfect through Christ. His sacrifice has redeemed you, covering every flaw and imperfection, and offering you the freedom to live a life of excellence and purpose. Your worth is not determined by the opinions of others or the ever-changing standards of the world. You don't have to live your life through the eyes of others, striving for their approval or validation. Instead, you can rest in the unshakable truth that God sees you as whole, cherished, and complete. In His eyes, you are already perfect—loved beyond measure and created with intention.

Because of Christ, you have the power to live boldly and confidently, reflecting the excellence of your Creator. You are called to live a life of joy, purpose, and faith, knowing that His grace is sufficient for every step of your journey. Each affirmation in this book is a tool to help you walk in the truth of your identity, to silence self-doubt, and to embrace the extraordinary person God created you to be. Let these words guide you as you grow in faith, trust in His plan, and shine His light in the world around you.

Living a life of excellence doesn't mean striving for perfection by human standards. It means walking in alignment with God's will, trusting His purpose, and allowing His Spirit to lead you. It means knowing that you are enough because of Christ and stepping into each day with the assurance that you are fully loved, equipped, and chosen for great things. When challenges arise, let these affirmations remind you of God's faithfulness and His unchanging love for you.

As you move forward, let the truth of these affirmations shape the way you see yourself and others. Embrace your gifts, lean into His promises, and know that you are a vessel of His grace and love. You are not defined by your past or the expectations of others—you are defined by the Creator who calls you His own. You are perfect in His eyes, and through Him, you can live a life of excellence that reflects His glory.

Prayer to Close the Journey:
Lord, thank You for creating me in Your image and making me perfect through Christ. Help me to live boldly in the truth of who I am in You. Let me walk confidently, not in the eyes of the world, but in the assurance of Your love. Strengthen my faith, guide my steps, and help me to reflect Your excellence in all that I do. In Jesus' name, Amen.

Practical Ways to Build Self-Esteem

Building self-esteem is a journey that requires intentional effort and practical steps to see yourself through God's eyes. Here are everyday strategies to help you grow in confidence, heal from past wounds, and embrace your worth:

1. Seek Therapy to Unpack Childhood Trauma
Sometimes, low self-esteem is rooted in experiences from your past. If you grew up in an environment filled with criticism, neglect, or hurtful words, these experiences can leave lasting scars. Therapy is a safe space to explore and process those feelings. A trusted therapist can help you unpack the impact of your childhood, reframe negative beliefs, and learn healthy ways to move forward. Remember, seeking help is not a sign of weakness but of strength and courage.

2. Change the Soundtrack of Your Mind
If you've grown up hearing negativity or criticism, it's time to change the soundtrack. Replace those harmful words with life-giving truths. Start by identifying the lies you've believed about yourself and counter them with affirmations based on Scripture, such as "I am fearfully and wonderfully made" (Psalm 139:14).

Another powerful way to reframe your mindset is through music. Choose a song that speaks to the person you want to become or reflects God's promises for your life. Play it when you need encouragement, and let it remind you of the truth about who you are in Christ. Songs like "You Say" by Lauren Daigle or "No Longer Slaves" by Bethel Music can be a great start.

3. Practice Daily Gratitude
Each day, write down three things you're grateful for. Gratitude shifts your focus from what's lacking to the blessings in your life. As you cultivate a thankful heart, you'll begin to see yourself and your circumstances in a more positive light.

4. Set Small, Achievable Goals
Boost your confidence by setting and accomplishing small goals. Whether it's completing a task, learning something new, or helping someone, every achievement reinforces your ability to succeed and reminds you of your strengths.

5. Surround Yourself with Positive People
The company you keep matters. Spend time with people who encourage and uplift you, those who reflect God's love and remind you of your worth. Positive relationships build a strong foundation for healthy self-esteem.

6. Speak Life Over Yourself
Words have power. Each day, speak affirmations out loud, such as:

- "I am loved and chosen by God."
- "I am worthy of love and respect."
- "I can do all things through Christ who strengthens me."
  Hearing these truths repeatedly will help you internalize them.

7. Spend Time in God's Presence
Prayer, worship, and reading God's Word are essential for grounding your identity in Christ. Allow Him to renew

your mind and remind you of your purpose. Spend a few minutes each day reflecting on Scriptures that affirm your value and uniqueness.

8. Celebrate Your Progress
Building self-esteem is a process, not an overnight transformation. Celebrate every step forward, no matter how small. Each victory, no matter how minor, is proof of growth and God's work in your life.

These practical steps, rooted in faith and intentional living, will help you replace self-doubt with confidence and step boldly into the person God created you to be. Remember, you are worthy, loved, and perfect in His eyes.

The Thought Jar - Renewed Minds Therapy Services

The Thought Jar, offered by Renewed Minds Therapy Services, is an innovative digital platform designed to help individuals recognize and identify negative thoughts, emotions, and actions. This app serves as a valuable tool for tracking your thought patterns over time, making it easier to spot recurring negative or self-defeating thoughts.

When using The Thought Jar, you log your thoughts, feelings, or emotions into the app, labeling them as positive, negative, or neutral. Based on your input, the app drops a green marble for positive thoughts, a yellow marble for neutral thoughts, and a red marble for negative thoughts. It then categorizes your thought into cognitive distortions such as "overgeneralization" or "catastrophizing," helping you understand the nature of your thinking patterns.

The app also features a glossary of terms related to thoughts, feelings, and actions, allowing you to deepen your understanding of the psychological concepts at play. With the ability to reframe negative thoughts into more positive or neutral alternatives, The Thought Jar becomes an essential resource for cultivating healthy mental habits and fostering personal growth. It can be found at www.theselfcaresanctuary.com

Renew Your Mind Thought Journal: A 13 Week Journey to Mindfulness and Self- Discovery

"Renew Your Mind Thought Journal" is a transformative 13-week journey designed to enhance self-awareness, positivity, and personal growth. Authored by Terri McColl, a seasoned mental health therapist and counselor, this journal offers a collection of thought-provoking prompts and affirmations to guide readers through reflections on various aspects of life.

Structured around themes like self-belief, resilience, gratitude, and embracing change, each week presents new prompts to inspire introspection and encourage the cultivation of healthy habits. Terri McColl's expertise in mental health and counseling shines through as she guides readers to explore their thoughts, emotions, and aspirations, fostering a deeper connection to themselves and their inner strengths.

With its comprehensive approach to self-discovery, "Renew Your Mind Thought Journal" empowers readers to embark on a meaningful journey of growth, self-care, and positive transformation. Ideal for those seeking to improve their mental well-being and live a more fulfilling life, this journal serves as a supportive companion for anyone dedicated to renewing their mind and embracing a more positive outlook.

Rise & Thrive: A 90 Day Selfcare Planner

Rise and Thrive is a transformative 90-day self-care planner designed to help you prioritize your well-being, nurture your mental health, and cultivate a more balanced, fulfilling life. This planner is your companion on a journey toward greater self-awareness, emotional regulation, and personal growth.

Each section of the planner is thoughtfully designed to guide you through the process of self-care, helping you to develop and maintain habits that enhance your mental, emotional, and physical well-being. By engaging with these tools daily, you'll learn to identify and manage your triggers, cultivate gratitude, and embrace a more mindful and balanced lifestyle.

Whether you are new to self-care or looking to deepen your practice, Rise and Thrive provides a structured yet flexible approach to nurturing yourself. As you complete the planner, you will gain valuable insights into your personal needs and preferences, empowering you to continue prioritizing your health and happiness long after the 90 days have passed.

Take each day one step at a time, embrace the power of self-care, and discover the strength within you to rise and thrive. This planner is not just a book, but a journey towards a healthier, happier you.

Tranquil Escapes: A Colorful Journey to Relaxation and Renewal

Within these pages, alongside calming designs, discover uplifting quotes carefully curated to inspire and empower. Let the words resonate as you color, fostering a positive mindset. As you bring each page to life with your unique palette, may these motivational quotes serve as beacons of encouragement, guiding you through moments of self-reflection and reinforcing the strength within. 'Tranquil Escapes' is not just a coloring book; it's a journey towards renewal, reminding you that amidst every stroke of color, there's a canvas of resilience waiting to unfold.

Coloring can trigger the brain's relaxation response, signaling safety and reducing the activation of the stress response system. When engaged in a calming activity like coloring, the brain shifts from a state of hyperarousal to a more balanced and relaxed state. The repetitive and rhythmic motions involved in coloring activate the parasympathetic nervous system, promoting a sense of safety and well-being. This calming effect is associated with the release of neurotransmitters like serotonin, which contributes to a positive mood and a feeling of security. Overall, coloring serves as a powerful tool to communicate to the brain that the immediate environment is non-threatening, fostering a sense of safety and calmness.

Mindful Progress: A Guided Journal for Mental Health Talk Therapy

"Mindful Progress" is a meticulously crafted guided journal that invites individuals to embark on a transformative journey of self-discovery, personal growth, and healing. Authored by Terri McColl, a seasoned mental health therapist and entrepreneur, this journal is a dynamic tool designed to support individuals navigating their therapeutic process.

With a comprehensive range of activities and prompts, "Mindful Progress" provides a holistic approach to self-improvement. From tracking therapy appointments and daily moods to engaging with reflective prompts and transition reflections, the journal offers a versatile toolkit for fostering mindfulness and self-awareness. Each week presents opportunities for progress tracking and growth assessment, guided by Terri's compassionate insights.

"Mindful Progress" is more than a mere journal; it's a roadmap for growth and transformation. With Terri McColl's compassionate guidance, readers are empowered to navigate their personal journeys with intention. Whether tracking progress, embracing mindfulness, or fostering self-compassion, this journal serves as a supportive companion, inspiring individuals to harness their inner strength and embrace positive change.

From the reflective prompts to the weekly wrap-up reflections, "Mindful Progress" serves as a reminder that every step taken toward well-being is a testament to resilience and personal empowerment. Through Terri McColl's expertise and compassionate approach, the journal encapsulates the essence of a healing and transformative process, guiding individuals towards a more mindful and empowered version of themselves.

Put Your Lid Down: Overcoming Childhood Trauma and Reclaiming Emotional Stability

Childhood trauma leaves a lasting impact, affecting emotional regulation, mental health, and relationships well into adulthood. *Put Your Lid Down* offers a comprehensive roadmap for healing, focusing on reclaiming emotional control and moving from survival to thriving. Drawing from neuroscience, psychology, and personal experience, the book explains how trauma disrupts brain function and emotional regulation, particularly through the metaphor of "flipping your lid," where the emotional brain takes over, leaving rational thought behind.

The book begins by defining trauma and exploring its long-term effects, including anxiety, depression, and emotional numbness. Trauma survivors often find themselves stuck in emotional patterns shaped by early life experiences. Understanding these patterns is the first step toward breaking free from them.

The book introduces the neuroscience behind emotional dysregulation, showing how trauma keeps the brain in a state of heightened alert, making it difficult to manage emotions and think clearly. It explains how unresolved trauma affects decision-making, relationships, and well-being, leading to chronic emotional distress.

A key focus is on reconnecting with the inner child—the part of you that still carries the pain and survival instincts from childhood. By acknowledging and comforting this inner child, you begin to heal those old wounds and release the hold trauma has on your present life.

Put Your Lid Down provides practical strategies for emotional healing, divided into two main areas: cognitive-behavioral techniques and mind-body approaches. Cognitive-behavioral strategies help reframe negative thoughts and challenge irrational beliefs, while mind-body techniques, such as mindfulness, physical exercise, creative outlets, and faith-based practices, help calm the nervous system and foster emotional balance.

A unique tool introduced in the book is "The Thought Jar," an app developed by the author that helps users track and reframe negative thoughts. This tool serves as a practical extension of cognitive-behavioral therapy, empowering users to monitor their thought patterns and cultivate healthier mental habits.

The book also emphasizes the importance of building a supportive social network and finding strength in faith. For the author, faith in God is a cornerstone of healing, providing reassurance, guidance, and a sense of peace during the recovery process.

As readers progress through the book, they are guided toward a new understanding of emotional control, moving from a state of constant vigilance to one of calm and clarity. The book encourages self-compassion, patience, and personal growth as readers learn to put their "lid down," allowing their prefrontal cortex to regain control over emotional responses.

Put Your Lid Down concludes with a message of hope, reminding readers that healing is possible and within reach. By addressing trauma, retraining the brain, and embracing personal growth, readers can transform their lives from surviving to truly thriving. This book provides the tools and insights needed to reclaim emotional stability, foster resilience, and build a future filled with possibilities.

The Self-Care Sanctuary

About Terri McColl

Terri McColl is a highly respected Licensed Clinical Professional Counselor (LCPC) licensed in Maryland and a dedicated Professional School Counselor for Prince George's County Public Schools. With a passion for mental health and a commitment to supporting individuals on their journey to healing, Terri has become a trusted resource for those seeking growth and emotional well-being.

As the owner of Renewed Minds Therapy Services, Terri specializes in childhood trauma, addiction, depression, and anxiety, providing tailored therapeutic interventions that promote lasting change. Her experience spans over 15 years, during which she has cultivated expertise in a variety of therapeutic modalities, ensuring that her approach aligns with the unique needs of each client.

A proud graduate of Bowie State University, Terri integrates both her academic background and extensive experience into her practice. She is also a sought-after speaker, frequently contributing to mental health discussions, including as a presenter at Faith City Central's annual Mental Health Awareness Conference.

Terri's approach to therapy is both compassionate and solution-focused, always aiming to empower her clients to tap into their strengths and navigate life's challenges with confidence. With her dedication to fostering growth and resilience, Terri McColl continues to be a beacon of hope and transformation for those she serves.

The Self-Care Sanctuary

Begin your journey to healing, self-care, and renewal today. At **The Self-Care Sanctuary**, we offer a comprehensive range of services designed to nurture your mind, body, and soul, all in one place. Whether you are seeking therapeutic support through **Renewed Minds Therapy Services** or looking to elevate your self-care routine, we are here to guide you every step of the way.

Visit www.theselfcaresanctuary.org and www.renewedmindstherapy.com to explore the full spectrum of offerings. Discover how our compassionate therapists can help you navigate childhood trauma, depression, anxiety, and life transitions with personalized therapy plans.

Enhance your self-care with our **Hotel Collection for Aromatherapy**, featuring luxurious essential oil blends to uplift your spirit. Reflect and grow with our **Mindful Progress Journal, Thought Jar**, and **The Renew Your Mind Thought Journal**—tools designed to inspire and foster emotional well-being. Pamper yourself at **Polish'd Nail Salon and Hair Studio** and embrace the art of self-care in every aspect of your life.

Your journey to renewal and transformation begins now. Explore our sanctuary of healing and empowerment today.

Perfect in His Eyes: Faith-Filled Affirmations from A-Z to Build Self-Esteem

In a world that often challenges self-worth, *Perfect in His Eyes* is a heartwarming guide for teenage Christian girls or anyone struggling with self-esteem. This inspiring book weaves together positive affirmations, therapeutic insights, and foundational Christian principles to remind readers of their unique value and purpose as children of God.

Organized from A to Z, each entry highlights a specific affirmation, paired with uplifting words and a carefully chosen Bible verse. From "Loved" to "Zealous," these affirmations empower readers to embrace their identity in Christ, overcome self-doubt, and walk confidently in the truth of God's promises. The book offers encouragement for every letter of the alphabet, helping girls see themselves through the eyes of their Creator.

Perfect in His Eyes is more than a book—it's a companion for any young woman seeking to grow in faith, self-love, and purpose. By embracing these affirmations, readers will discover the joy of living boldly, rooted in the unwavering love and grace of God.